FRANCE
MASSIF CENTRAL
Stephen Platt

www.leveretpublishing.com

France: Massif Central
First published - September 2024
Published by Leveret Publishing
56 Covent Garden, Cambridge, CB1 2HR, UK

Wild narcissus pocking through the snow

ISBN 978-1-912460-68-7

© Stephen Platt 2024

All rights reserved. No part of this publication may be reproduced, stored in a retrieval system or transmitted in any form by any means, electronic, mechanical, photocopying, recording or otherwise, except brief extracts for the purpose of review, without the written permission of the publisher.

MASSIF CENTRAL 2024

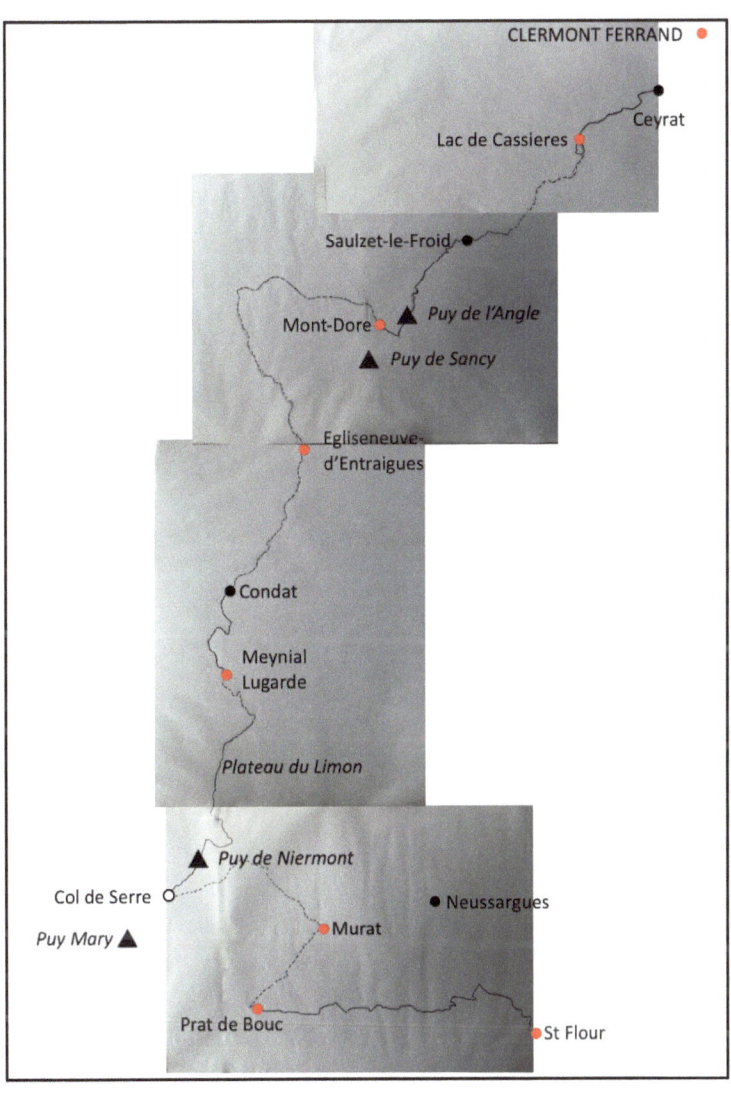

The Journey Hathersage to France

Monday, Tuesday 29-30 April 2024

It was an easy journey to London from Hathersage and the Belgrove Hotel where I am staying is only two minutes from St Pancras. The hotel is spartan, but it's clean and conveniently near the station.

The early evening is sunny and warm in the square between Kings Cross and St Pancras and I stroll through the new development and walk around Camley Street Nature Park that I'd seen from the train. I cross the foot bridge near St Pancras lock and find a wine bar, the Porte Noir, housed in one of the old circular gas holders next to the Regent's Canal. I order a butternut squash risotto, that turns out to be delicious, and an expensive glass of Chablis.

I woke in the night worried about an email that I'd opened saying I'd won Euros 680,000, about half a million pounds, on the French lottery. I'm

Camley Street Nature Park

sure it's a fraud and that I've downloaded some malware. Nevertheless I can't help musing about how I'd spend it. I could divide it amongst the grand-children or give it away to charity. Maybe I'd give it all to Corpus, my old college. Or I could rent a beach house and spend the winters somewhere warm. The fraudsters seem to have gone to a lot of trouble creating a French lottery certificate and giving the name of the person I should contact to claim my prize in the Standard Chartered Bank in Paris. I found their address and emailed them but got no reply. When I got home I rang the bank and they confirmed it was a scam. I wonder how many calls they had to field and what was in it for the fraudsters.

I shower and get to the station early and spend an hour people gazing, noting the types and colours of people's luggage.

Paris is quite different to London and I realise why some foreign visitors say that it's dirty. The stations the Gare du Nord and the Gare du Lyon haven't had the makeover of St Pancras, Kings Cross and the other London mainline stations.

There is a 10-minute walk from the Gare de Lyon to the Gare de Bercy. The route goes past the Olympic Stadium, from the outside a rather ugly

Regents Canal and King Cross development

building relieved by steep grass walls that look difficult to mow. Yet two months later watching the Olympics on the TV it looked fantastic. There are a row of food shops and an enticing boulangerie catches my eye, and I buy a slice of Quiche Lorraine, and a ham and cheese sandwich.

The train to Clermont Ferrand is delayed half an hour, supposedly because a young man hasn't paid his fare and is taken off the train and arrested. It seemed a little excessive for a misdemeanour, but perhaps there was more to it. There's a large station in Clermont Ferrand and I have time to kill before the train to Neussargues. Rather than try and find a seat in the crowded station I venture forth and walk through the old town looking for the Old Ravel Hotel, where I plan to stay on the way back home. It's near the local covered market and looks ethnic with its brightly coloured paint and tile work. There's nowhere to sit when I get back to the station so I go outside to the concourse and sit on one of the stone benches and watch people arriving for trains on their scooters, steaming across the concourse at high speed and hopping off at the last minute in front of the main doors.

I leave it a little late to go for my train. It's a single carriage and full of

Olympic stadium, Paris

people standing. I push on into the carriage, passed all the bikes in the doorway. There's a double bass occupying the only vacant place. We set off and a young lady offers me her seat. I try to refuse, saying it'll all be fine but she insists and I sit with a mixture of relief at getting a seat and a sense of mortification. I was taken by her generosity since she said she was going to the end of the line in Aurillac. This is a little local train stopping at every village and even more people get on at the next two stops. Finally people began to disembark and the generous young lady got a seat.

The train passes through a plain of severely pollarded lime and plane trees before entering the narrow gorge of the River Allanche, it's steep granite walls glistening black, a round castle high above on the top of the cliffs. The rail line and narrow road hug the river and pass through cuttings and tunnels.

Some way before we get to Neussargues I ring a local taxi firm and arrange to be picked up. The station is wonderfully clean and modern but the toilet is locked so I explore round the back of the railway sheds and find somewhere to pee. A flock of Goldfinch land in the trees.

Cedric of Charbonnel Taxi arrives and I sit in the front on the drive to

Rail station Clermont Ferrand

Saint Flour because his son us in the back. He asks if I live en ville ou à la campagne and whether the Peak District is arable or pasture. I tell him that my home is in a national park somewhat similar to the Massif Central. We talk about the weather. I assume it is particularly bad this week, but he says it is always like this the end of April and the start of May. He drops me at the Hotel d'Etape, saying it has a very good restaurant, and so it proves. The room was nice and I washed and went down to a dinner of fresh fish followed by sorbet and ice cream.

Pont Vieux, St Flour (1845)

Day 1 Sant Flour to Prat de Bouc

Wednesday 1 May 28km

I slept well and, after a light breakfast and having made a baguette sandwich for lunch, set off in the rain. Saint Flour is much bigger and grander than I expected. It's in two parts. My hotel was in the lower town and after crossing the old stone bridge over the river, the path climbs steeply to the Citadel and the upper town. This must have been an important place in the past, at the confluence of two rivers, on the important route south.

I feel tired and sluggish slogging up the narrow lane, the Rue de Thuile Bas, following the Calvary that rises up to the Citadel with a panorama view of the town.

They are relaying the paving in the main square with small triangles of pale rough black tufa and white granite. The tufa is good to walk on in the

Cathédrale Saint-Pierre de Saint-Flour

rain because it's rough and my boots grip well. The area in front of the cathedral and the Marie is unfinished and someone must have walked across when the cement was newly laid because there is a line of footprints.

It's a lovely town – well-kept with lots of prosperous working shops. The path descends steeply to where it crosses the railway line and the river. They are laying new track, taking up the short lengths of rail on wooden sleepers and replacing with much longer lengths on concrete sleepers. The way is barred and there is a sign saying no access. I continue anyway and am climbing a wire fence when I see a rail worker in orange high vis coming towards me. Distracted, I catch my foot as I stretch over the fence and fall sprawling. I scramble to my feet and cross the track anyway. I climb the second fence and set off down the road, Massales, crossing a stone bridge across the River Ander and pass another sign barring the way from the other direction.

The path goes due west, crossing lush grassland with the small herds of Charolais cattle each with a watchful bull. One particular mahogany coloured Salers bull comes towards the fence, bellowing and shaking his

Salers bull

long horns at me while another group of young bulls scatter as soon as I take my camera out to get a shot. I don't know if any of the photos will come out since the phone is soaked and the lens is covered in water.

You pass a succession of hamlets, the first, Saint-Cirgues d'Andelat, has a covered bench seat where I can get out of the rain and a modern toilet right in front of the Marie. It gives me the wrong idea since none of the subsequent villages are anywhere near as well appointed. The church, which dates from 1229, has a walled bell tower that houses 4 bells open to the skies but alas is bordered up and there is no way to see inside.

The way is fairly flat and straight and the road paved with gravel. The first part winds its way through woodland to skirt a river valley passing a series of horse paddocks. Then it becomes muddy and broken. Maybe they have been felling trees and the lorries have churned up the path. There are signs saying the way is barred and it is prohibited to pedestrians. As usual, I ignored the sign and press on, picking my way through the quagmire, trying to keep my boots dry. But the rain is relentless, and I can feel myself getting damp.

At Le Sailhant there is a romantic thousand-year-old fortified chateau

Église Saint-Cirgues d'Andelat

Trompe-l'œil on the door of a barn

Strange contraption for restraining calves?

Village bread oven

Grassy ramp up to first floor

perched on the rocky remains of a basalt outcrop. It's now owned by an America, Joseph Pell Lombardi, a Preservation Architect. The Cascade de Barbory is a little further upstream from the stone bridge across the river.

The next village is Mons, then at about one o'clock, in the village of Liozargues, I am on the lookout for somewhere to stop and finally find an open garage and an up-turned pail out of the rain to sit on to eat my sandwich.

All the villages look well maintained and the roads are well kept without potholes, and whether from the EU or national government, this region seems to be well resourced. Many of the houses have small allotments and people keep hens and ducks. Every hamlet has a church and a redundant bread oven. They also have strange contraptions for restraining cattle consisting of covered stall with a yoke halter and iron hook at the tail end. Maybe it's for castrating bullocks. This rural economy is fascinating but opaque without more understanding. Anyway, it's all changed since the Second World War.

Even though Valuéjois seems quite large, everywhere is closed and I have to press on along gravelled farm tracks. There are crosses at intervals and

Chateau du Sailhant on its basalt outcrop

it looks like a pilgrimage way and maybe part of the Camino de Santiago. I've been tired all day, but now I'm struggling to keep going and it's tempting to explore a sign for a gite in the small hamlet of Lescure offering accommodation as I'm still two to three hours from Prat de Bouc, where I'm booked in for the night.

I press on to the Bois des Fraux. It's not clear where the path goes from here and I cast around, finally crossing under an electric fence into a boggy field, which seems to be more promising even though there is no sign at first of a path. I carry on and a faint path appears, rising steadily over grassland to a moor. It's misty and feels remote, isolated and committing.

It's raining and I'm wet and cold and very tired. I need a break but there's nowhere to stop, not even to perch. But I take off my sack anyway and find a nut bar and chew on it as I walk, spluttering peanut bits because I'm panting. The short stop and bit of food has revived me and I press on, using my sticks to make progress, pushing on my arms to help get over the humps in the moorland. I note a stone building in the distance and imagine a dry hay-filled barn and am tempted to go and explore, but I'm too tired to risk deviating from the path. The path levels and I pass a pile of stones

Chateau du Sailhant

with a cross and feel I'm getting there.

The path begins to descend, the mist clears and I can see down into the valley and catch a glimpse of the snow-covered slopes opposite. Finally I spot the ski resort at the Prat de Bouc and follow the steep winding track, stumbling on the stones, my toes and feet aching.

I go to the restaurant and am welcomed by a large Great Dane and a genial host. Julien says I'll dine here but the gîte is opposite. The guardienne, Annalise, is most welcoming and the gîte is wonderfully clean and warm and well-appointed. The room is fine and I take off my sodden clothes and have a shower. I imagine my trousers and top are dry enough and put them back on, thinking that they'll dry on me. The rest I put in the drying room.

I run to the restaurant in the rain and get the shakes over dinner. I've been looking forward to a pottage soup, but the starter is meaty, pâté and chorizo. There are two other guests, women who have come from Buron d'Eylac. They are on the second course – a slab of beef and boiled potatoes. It looks much too big a plate for me and I'm not feeling great. I'm shaking with cold and feeling nauseous. So I ask for a small portion and

Buron Prat de Bouc on a much nicer day than when I was there

even then I can eat less than half and refuse the sweet. Julien is marvellously understanding and I pay up and sneak off to bed and sleep till seven o'clock.

Interior of Buron Prat de Bouc

Day 2 Prat de Bouc to Murat

Thursday 2 May

Breakfast is excellent – coffee, juice, muesli, bread and jam, and cake. I pack up and clear the room and settle in the sitting room to wait for Annalise. It's snowing outside and I ask the young women about Buron d'Eylac. They say the refuge is cold and the wood is wet and I'll need a lighter because the matches are damp. The local auberge might provide a meal, but it isn't certain. My hips and feet ache and I'm struggling to walk with stiff legs, so I decide on a rest day and inquire about a bus to the nearest town – Murat. There is no bus but Julien says Annalise will take me when she finishes clearing. So I have a coffee in the restaurant Buron and look online for somewhere to stay. I find a place advertising itself a "Charmant appartement au cœur des volcans d Auvergne" and book.

Annalise bustles in just after midday saying she's ready. She has a van, and on the way down to Murat a chamois walks across the road and is

L'Arôme Antique guest house Murat.

away before I can raise my phone to take a photo. I ask her about her life and if she's always lived here. She says that she was born in Murat and her mother lives here still, but after leaving school, she was desperate to leave. She has lived in Peru and Sri Lanka and Galway and other places and worked as a translator, a mountain ski instructor and many other things. "I have two boys of 18 and 20 but no husband", she says.

Soon we are driving up the main street to the square where they are resurfacing the paving. Annalise says they're doing this everywhere and doesn't seem pleased. She finds my hotel. It's opposite the Église Notre-Dame-des-Oliviers de Murat, a delightful building with a stone roof like fish scales.

It's only one o'clock and Michael, my host, says he needs an hour or so to clean the room. So I wander around the steep narrow streets taking in the lay of the land. From a high vantage point I can look down on the town. There are two factories and I can hear the hum of machinery. I discover that one makes filtration media from rock and the other is a flour mill, Les Moulins d'Antoine, one of the largest in France, milling wheat from around Clermont Ferrand. There's a rocky outcrop with a White Virgin

Place du Planol

and Child that seem about to jump. I stop at a vantage point and watch a kite soaring and stooping majestically over the town, covering the distance to the outcrop in a couple of seconds.

I pop into a cafe in the main square and have a portion of moussaka and a tea until Michael calls and says the room is ready. It's a comfortable large apartment and Michael stops to chat. He says his mother came from Halifax and met his father, a Tunisian Jew, in Switzerland. His mother now lives in the south of France where Michael was born. I say the apartment has a North African feel. Michael also spent time in Ireland and his English is good. He says he always wanted to run a restaurant and he and his brother renovated this place and set up the business but his brother was killed in a motorbike accident. He's lovely, but looks careworn as if he doesn't sleep well, and he's very thin.

After a rest I go down to dinner. There are people in the bar and I have to push past but Michael has laid a table for me with the view of the church roof. He asks what I want and I ask for soup. It looks doubtful and then he says he has some carrots. That's followed by risotto. Michael is a good cook.

Michael proprietor of the L'Arôme Antique

Tower of Église Notre-Dame-des-Oliviers de Murat

Street market in front of La Halle, Murat

Our-Lady-of-the-High-Auvergne looks ready to jump

View from Col de Serre towards Le Puy Mary

Puy de Niermont (1620m)

Day 3 Murat to Meynial Lugarde

Friday 3 May 24km

Today is a good day. It's dry for once and Michael asked about plans. "I am thinking to get a taxi to Col de Serre and join the path there. I'm in luck, he says he'll give me a lift once he's cleared up.

I get a quick glimpse of the open market in front of the church before getting into his white van to climb the steep narrow street past the bottom of the rock with the virgin. He says there used to be a castle, but that Cardinal Richelieu and the French Army demolished it in 1633 after the local lord sided with the British. Apparently it took six months and a lot of dynamite.

We pass through lush countryside and Michael tells me that there are still wolves and he saw one leaping across the road. He relates the legend of the beast that was finally killed long ago, that turned out to be a huge

Plateau de Limon

wolf. He tells me that the local cattle, the long horned brown cows I've been seeing along the way, are a Salers breed.

Quite soon we all up the col. We say goodbye and I set off up a grassy ridge towards the Puy de Niermont (1620m). It's uphill but not impossibly steep and I climb steadily. There is fresh snow on the ramped traverse to the summit. From here the path descends gradually, the land opening up to the vast Plateau de Limon, also called the Les Quiroux.

There is snow and the tracks of a hare, which I follow, subconsciously assuming that it knows the way. The snow isn't too deep and it's fairly easy going across the top of tussocky grass. There are deep muddy tractor tracks and the ground is soft from all the rain. This is a deep fertile loam so it cuts up badly. I come to a swollen stream that looks difficult to cross and the wire fence is wobbly and stops me jumping at the narrowest point. So I sit on a pile of rocks in the mud and take off my boots and socks and wade across.

I join a farm track. Stone barns dot the hillsides, but there are no cows in the meadows since they haven't been brought up from the lowlands. One or two of the stone buildings are labeled Buron on the map and

Farmhouse

St Saturnin

Anna in the bar at St Saturnin

Michael told me that these where were they made cheese.

French fighter planes have been flying high. Then a pair of majestic eagles soar up the narrow valley to my left. There is a wet path along a hedgerow and the path is deep sunk under ancient trees. There are wildflowers everywhere and it would be delightful if it wasn't so wet.

In Saint Saturnin I look longingly through the windows of a bar. It says it opens at 4.30; it's four now. A woman comes to the door and welcomes me in. She says she's only visiting and doesn't know the area. Her husband is a retired doctor and has taken the bar for the summer as a recreation. She's from Brittany and points to a picture on the wall showing Atlantic breakers on a broken shore. "Five weeks is enough and I'm going home soon. He'll stay on maybe", she says. "We travel a lot and we're going to the Greek islands in June and to the Seychelles later. I like swimming and snorkelling and I adore skiing in the Alps".

Her name is Anna when I ask for tea, she's flustered. She says she has nothing to offer. I have a tea bag, I say. And so she boils water and I have a reviving cup of tea. I'm not looking forward to the last four miles to Lugarde, so I try thumbing a lift in the square and a young woman stops.

Lugarde

Purple orchids (Orchis mascula) or Dead man's fingers

Bois de Font Sainte

Her name is Alex and she kindly takes me all the way to Lugarde, even though it's a little out of her way and she's meeting friends.

From the centre of Lugarde It's a short walk to Meynial. Eventually I find the gite but it looks closed and there is no one around. The skies suddenly most threatening and I cast around for shelter, finally finding a wood store and ring the number for the Gite Francais, the managing agents. They say they'll contact the proprietor and ring me back. I'm not confident but am pleasantly surprised when the ring to say that the keys are under the mat at the front door. And so they are.

I switch on the electric heaters because its cold in the stone cottage and I'm chilled from sitting out in the rain. I have the whole place to myself. It sleeps six and it's quite expensive but I couldn't find anything else.

I unpack and head back to Lugarde to find something to eat. Google reports that the bar is very friendly and run by Sergio, who's like an uncle. But everyone seems completely nonplussed when I ask for something to eat and they say they only serve drinks. The bar is more of a social centre for locals. They say there's a shop in Condat. I looked on the map. It's a long way and I'm too tired and anyway I wouldn't get there before it

Meynial Lugarde

closed. A young man and his girlfriend offer to take me. Matthew and Fedora are just back from an eight-month trip of 40 countries finishing in Georgia on are staying with his father at his holiday house. They take me to the local Carrefour supermarket. I'm just in time as it's about to close. I buy too much because I'm feeling hungry. On the way back they talk about the joys of travel and the problem of coming back and what to do next.

Back at the gite I make soup and add lentils from lunch but the paella with chicken makes my stomach heave and I'm sick. I've been finding it increasingly difficult to eat and keep down food and I'm worried what's wrong with me. Perhaps it's just exhaustion. I know I need the protein, but I can't face meat – the idea of eating flesh revolts me. The bed is comfortable, however, and I get a good night's sleep.

Cuckoo flower or Lady's smock (Cardamine pratensis)

Day 4 Meynial Lugarde to Egliseneuve-d'Entraigues

Saturday 4 May 21 km

The day dawns brighter than forecast and it isn't raining but I feel weak, maybe from lack of food and so I have a lazy start and don't get away till after 10am. First, I have the cream caramel I bought yesterday with a little bread and I make a goat cheese sandwich for lunch. I have to leave behind some of the food I bought yesterday.

The start is a mile or so of tarmac road before the path enters a forest – the Bois de Font Sainte. The path is churned with tractor tracks where it's muddy or there is water. I enter the forest and push through the undergrowth. Wildflowers are out. Using the app on my phone I find lady's bedstraw, wood anemone, hellebore, bittercress, cuckoo flower, purple orchid and oxlips.

This would be a lovely path if it wasn't for the tractor churning. I

Condat and Sam's bar for pizza lunch

wonder why the farmer drives down here, maybe to the shops or the garage in town? I cross a mountain stream and reach the road and another mile of tedious tarmac to the hamlet of Feniers where the path goes left, initially on a gravel track than a delightfully narrow woodland trail, dry and pleasant all the way to Condat. I cross the bridge and find a cafe called Sam. I order cafe au lait. The patron says it's Saturday and all they do is pizza or burger so I order a vegetarian pizza and a beer. The patron and his wife seem a little surly at first, but warm up after I order. Perhaps they are used to walkers not ordering lunch.

I'm tired and I've had enough for the day but it's another 10 or 12 miles to a Egliseneuve where I'm booked into the auberge. So I wait at the traffic island and hitch. A friendly man with a Mohican haircut and a Mexican moustache stops for me. He is an incredibly fast driver and I have visions of sliding off the wet road into a tree. It doesn't brake on the bends and just powers through. He must know the road really well.

The gite is closed. A girl with a huge pack is mooching around wondering what to do. She is doing the GR 30 and is having a hard time. I call the number for the gite and the man comes in 10 minutes and lets us

Hitch hiking in Condat

in. He's jovial and friendly, also called Michael, and says dinner is 7.30. I ask for a vegetarian and he produces a starter with eggs from his own hens and a salad followed by a delicious lentil curry and rice. Presented most beautifully, moulded into a cube for the rice and a cylinder of the curry, all washed down with a bottle of Rose.

Egliseneuve-d'Entraigues outside the Auberge la Grange

Day 5 Egliseneuve-d'Entraigues to Mont-Dore

Sunday 5 May 26 km

I sleep well on a comfortable bed in the most eccentric room with bright red architraves and pale blue doors. Michael offers to give me a lift if I can leave at 8.30 after breakfast, so I am up early and packed. Breakfast is the usual juice and eggs and homemade jams of plum and myrtle. The lift took nearly an hour, which was so generous of him.

The Alti'Pic hotel was most welcoming. It was just after 10 but Emily let me into the room and I had a rest before exploring. The plan was to reconnoitre the trail via the Gran Cascade to the Col de la Croix St Robert where the GR4 crossed before climbing to the Puy de l'Angle.

The Chemin de Poets starts almost opposite the hotel and after a short stretch of road and a path rears up steeply in a series of bends. I'm going okay with a light sack and enjoying the freedom of less weight, even

Mont-Dore from the Chemin de Poets

Le Capucin Mont-Dore

Gran Cascade on path to Col de la Croix St Robert

though it's steep and I'm breathing hard.

The cascade is spectacular and worth the climb. It's obviously a popular walk and there are lots of walkers, some with young children. From the cascade it gets even steeper and then there's a steel stairway. Finally the path opens up onto delightful moorland clothed in narcissus and the sun comes out and it's warm and pleasant. Such a contrast to the previous days.

The path curves across the moor running parallel to the road across the valley. It's easy walking now and much less steep, and I can look up to the Puy de l'Angle and weigh up the route tomorrow. It's 1,000-foot climb, zigzagging up the hillside that I think will be alright if the weather is kind.

I join the GR4 and do a circuit back to the cascade and stop before the staircase down and eat my lunch from yesterday – goats' cheese and tomato on rye, a little soggy from having sat in my rucksack.

It's pleasant going down, although hard on the knees and toes, and I take another path into the centre of the village and arrive at a large granite building with a sign saying Thermes. There's a patisserie and I buy a tea and a myrtle tart and sit in the sunshine in the square before walking back

Puy de L'Angle in the sunshine

Puy de Sancy from Tete de Flon

Gran Cascade

to the hotel.

Emily has booked me into the best restaurant in the village, L'Estavou. It's raining hard, but I walk quickly and don't get too wet. The restaurant is very French, small and intimate. And the food is superb. I have a goat's cheese starter. It reminds me of the time I walked out of a restaurant in Nantwich which was supposed to be good but all they had done was take the wrapper off a goat's cheese barrel and added a lettuce leaf. Here the cheese was melted on crusty bread and served with a salad dressed in delicious balsamic and honey. But the first course was surpassed by the main – perch, caught locally, and poached in wafer thin pastry and served with a trufflard of sliced potatoes in a delicious sauce and a compote of mixed vegetables. I had to refuse a dessert I was so full.

Thermal baths Mont-Dore

Day 6 Mont-Dore-Lac de Cassiere

Monday 6 May 26 km

It is raining hard as I get an early breakfast and make a sandwich for lunch. There is little traffic past the hotel and Emily says there's no chance of a lift and. It's misty with low cloud, slanting rain and a stiff breeze. So she calls a taxi which only takes 10 to 15 minutes to get to the col and the GR4. The weather is evil at the col. I disembark the warm vehicle and zip up my anorak and shoulder my pack. "Courage", says the woman chauffeur, giving me a wry smile as she climbs back in her cab and departs.

There is the mountain and the Puy de l'Angle, shrouded in thick cloud, so much more forbidding than in bright sunshine. Good job I sussed it yesterday, I thought as I set out. The start is boggy and the path goes straight up between wire fences making a narrow, muddy passage. I can't face wallowing around so I climb over the restraining wire and climb a grassy path to one side. I'm going well; slow but feeling good. The pace is

Église Sant Pardoux, Mont-Dore, in the rain

Puy de Barbier in the mist

Puy de la Tache

steady and I know I'll get there.

Higher up the path begins the big traverse left, so I know where I am, then it swings right and traverses the whole of the mountain, rising steadily in zigzags that get shorter until finally, I realise I'm getting to the top. There is a pile of rocks supporting the cross that can be seen from the col and, a little further on, the true summit with a tall pole. It's great to be at the top. The clouds swirl up from the west but there is an occasional break and I get a glimpse of the valleys below.

The path continuous to Puy Barbier and mercifully I get a glimpse back along the ridge. The clouds close in the path gets muddy and the ridge continues over four more Puys, each getting me puffing, but they're not too demanding. This will be marvellous in sunny dry weather. Never mind I'm here now.

Finally the path descends sharply to the Col Morand. It's tough on the knees and toes and I have to go carefully to avoid slipping on the wet stones and the broken steel steps that are lethal in the wet. But I get down safely and there is a restaurant, the Buron de Col, and I go in and find a log fire and soft leather sofas strewn with sheepskins. I take off my

Buron de Col Morand

Coffee in the Buron

GR4 to Passade

wet anorak and order a cafe au lait.

it's most pleasant lounging in front of the warm fire sipping my coffee. However, it's time to leave. It's midday and people are arriving in car parties for lunch. This is obviously a favourite spot. The cooking smells from the kitchen suggest this is a good place to eat. But I have a sandwich from breakfast and I need to get on.

There's a short stretch of road before a turnoff on a track, that gently descends to greener pastures of the flatlands – lush pastures clothed in dandelions and small sleepy villages. I get to Passade and catch up the two men from Paris who I've been leapfrogging since the col. They're going to Aydat and camping. Last night they were in a refuge on the Puy de le Tache above the col.

I decide to stop at a bench outside a bar, which I think is closed, and eat my baguette and cheese. But the owner comes out gives me a frosty stare and I realise that I've been rude sitting on his bench and not going in and ordering something. I try hitching as I don't fancy walking along the road, but there is no traffic. So I go on to Saulzet-le-Froid with its big church, but still there's no traffic. These are all little country roads and

Lush cow pastures

Aubrac cattle producing rich creamy milk for cheese making

Pessade village

although it's a weekday everywhere seems very sleepy.

I check the map and see that if I walk to Zanières there is a main road, the D5, going north to Lac de la Cassière where I'm booked in. It's another three kilometres but, despite being tired and footsore, I manage it okay and only have to hitch five minutes before a woman stops. She's Austrian, has lived in France 10 years, is married to a Rondoniere guide and has two sons. Her car is a mess and she's apologetic, moving stuff and making room for me. Her name is Terese and she chats on the 15 minute ride to the refuge, Entre Lacs et Volcans, where I'm staying.

It's only four o'clock and they don't open till five, but a man comes to the door and lets me in. Initially he's little cold and direct, but he warmed when we introduced ourselves I told him who I was where I had come from. His name is Serge. Dinner was excellent and he recommended a particular wine made by a friend of his.

Entre Lacs et Volcans, Cassière

Day 7 Lac de la Cassière

Tuesday 7 May 5 km

A restful day – breakfast then a walk around the lake on forest tracks once it stopped raining. Although it's wet in places the path is most pleasant because it's not bee churned up by tractors like so many of the other tracks I've been on. There is birdsong, cooing of doves in the distance and a cuckoo sounds across the valley. There are three or four small islands at the southern end of the lake – dark grey, jagged volcanic plugs poking out the water. There are signs saying private fishing but the path is public. The village seems somewhat deserted with obvious holiday homes and plenty of abandoned houses.

Hikers are camped by the side of the lake and are making lunch on small stoves in the drizzle. I wonder if they managed to stop here overnight or if this is a just lunch break and they are on the way to an official camping ground.

Lac de la Cassière and volcanic plugs

Back up the hotel it's time for a snooze before dinner. Tonight it's chicken casserole and rice with a spinach soup starter.

Lac de la Cassière

A renovation project

Day 8 Lac de la Cassière to Clermont Ferrand

Wednesday 8 May 12 km

After breakfast I settle up and say goodbye to Serge. I ask him about the business how many rooms they have and if they close in the winter. They have one dormitory of 6 beds, one of 4, and six doubles. There'll be busy from tomorrow, Victory Day in Europe and a national holiday. They open from the end of April to the end of September and then close for the winter. "It's not worth heating the whole place for one or two rooms", he says. In the winter they operate as a gite and families of twenty or so people can rent it for the Christmas period or New Year holidays.

They've been here three years. They used to run a restaurant and Serge likes cooking. He's been all over the world learning different cuisines including Sweden and Lapland. His English is good and he's able to communicate well. He says he likes to go foraging in the forest for plants and mushrooms.

"The people lived off the land in times past, for example during the war, he says. "My friend is very knowledgeable and has written a book, wonderfully illustrated, with all the wild plants of the Massif Central and their uses for food or medicine. We have people coming on courses and I take them out collecting plants which I cook, but the grandparents won't eat it because of the trauma of the war and having to survive on what they could forage."

I say that we've largely lost this peasant knowledge in Britain. "It's the same here", he says, "people have left and villages are empty. And weekenders don't have the understanding. But it's important we keep this knowledge alive. It may be important given all the change and turmoil in the world."

This gets Serge talking about the war and Brexit. "What a pity", he says, "we couldn't comprehend it." "Neither could we", I say. "Will there be another vote?" "Maybe. Labour wants to move closer to Europe. We shot ourselves in the foot." "That's what politicians do, it's the same here", he says. "They say one thing and do another, but we should be together. Like during the war when Charles de Gaulle was in London, broadcasting on the BBC, encouraging the resistance and providing hope to Free French. "de Gaulle and Churchill together against Nazism", Serge said wistfully. "Without them we'd be speaking German." "Yes, it was a close-run thing for a while. Had Britain being invaded the Americans may not have entered the war", I said. "England and France, we're like two brothers. Sometimes at odds, sometimes together." Serge is animated and his eyes shine with pleasure.

I ask about the skiing says that if you can ski here, you can ski anywhere. Children's start at three. There are no lifts. So it's all off-piste mountain skiing. The Massif Central catches the first depressions bringing snow from the Atlantic. But the snow is getting less each year. The tree line stops at 1,500 meters here and in the Alps at 2500. They have a cottage and when they close for five months in the winter they live there.

We shake hands and I set off. It's a bright sunny day with sharp nip in the air and I walk up to the main road and try hitching for a while. The plan is to walk to Ceyrat and catch a bus into the centre of Clermont

Gorge de Ceyrat, Ruisseau de St Genès

Ferrand. Buses are every hour or so, so there's no pressure to get there for a set time as the hotel doesn't open till four.

I try hitching for 10 minutes. It's a good place to stop and various cars go past but none stop. So I give up and walk along the main road a couple of miles to Thiers. Luckily there is a narrow grassy border on the other side of a low concrete barrier so I don't have to walk on the fast road.

At Thiers I turn off along a small rural road. The area looks prosperous, with large modern houses. People are buying bread at the local patisserie and greengrocers and it all looks very civilised. A stony bank is full of wildflowers, and succulents and I ponder about creating a green roof on top of Jack's cottage at Leveret Croft.

A man is exercising is horse where the gorge that leads to Ceyrat begins – the Ruisseau de St Genès. It's muddy so I hop over a fence and walk along the adjacent field till the path gets drier. It's most pleasant and easy walking for two or three miles along the gorge. I stop at a bridge and sit down on a stone abutment and eat my lunch of bread and cheese and an apple that I made a breakfast.

Sculpture in the Gorge de Ceyrat

This must be a popular walk because I meet various couples out for a passeo. I reached the road and turn towards the centre of Ceyrat and find the Marie and the bus stop after about a mile. I realised that the bus went all the way to the gorge where it turned around and that I could have caught it there. I had thought I would have an hour to wait but Google says that there is one in a few minutes.

It's hot in the sunshine, the first time I've been really warm on the trip so far. The bus into town is pleasant and I observe my fellow passengers and appreciate the virtues of a bus service for those without a car.

Clermont Ferrand and much bigger than I'd imagined. However, when I check it's much smaller than Sheffield. Apparently it's the home of Michelin tire. The hotel Ravel is delightful, much nicer than I expected, and there's a holiday atmosphere with it being Victory Day. The two barmen are chatting up a girl in tight pants, boots and a motorbike jacket. They're splashing the drinks about and getting very jolly. After all, it's a national holiday and very few other places seem open.

I order tea and mix the black tea bag with an Earl Grey t-bag I brought from breakfast. I dump my stuff in my room and go off exploring and find

a Spar and buy local produce to take home – saucisson, cheese, nougat and chocolate almonds. When I get back and I decide to try the jacuzzi. A couple are already in occupation but they make room. The pool is tiled and the water jets feel really powerful. So I stretch out and let the bubble ease my back and toes. It's delightfully warm. Sun pours into the space and it's almost delightful. So much better than I imagined.

In the bar I relax and enjoy just stopping and doing nothing. I ask the receptionist to recommend a restaurant but the two she tries are both full. It's a holiday after all and I realise I should have asked earlier. Finally she finds a table in the Brasserie Madeleine in the Place de la Victoire. How appropriate for Victory Day. It's 15-minute walk, but it's a beautiful sunny evening and it's good to see more of the town. There is an avenue with plane trees and cafes with men chatting and playing board games. They look like immigrants from Africa and the Middle East.

Google Maps leads me up a side street where there's a house with a sign saying Marshal of France. The alleyways have antique streetlamps casting a delightful glow and there is a stone fountain with children playing in the sunshine.

Rue de Blaise Pascal

Rue de l'Oratoire

Fountain in the Rue du Terrail

The Brasserie is perfect, right on the square in front of the cathedral. I order a glass of Chablis while perusing the menu, finally settling on a salad of large prawns and frites. It's marvellous if a bit messy peeling the crayfish with my fingers. The sun has set and it's getting chilly outside, so I set off back to the hotel following my nose rather than resorting to Google. The bar is welcoming and that barman suggests I try a local spirit as a 'digestive'. made from verbena – Liqueur de Verveine de Velay. He searches the shelves for the bottle and finally finds unopened. It's an unusual drink and I wonder if I should have ordered beer like the others in the bar.

There's plenty of noise from the bar so I use my earplugs. The pillow is hard and I wake in the night with them hurting so I take them out. Mercifully, the hotel and street are quiet now and I sleep

Bar staff in the Old Hotel Ravel

Day 9 Clermont Ferrand to Home

Thursday 9 May

I breakfast pack. settle up and have a final coffee before heading to the station and the train to Paris. It's not long to wait and leaves on time. It's a beautiful sunny day, the best of the whole trip. Not surprising since this is the day I Leave. But it's been a great holiday, relaxing in a way and a new different area to get to know. I rather liked the mixed mode less purist form of travel, getting lifts over the difficult bits or when I was tired. I realise it was badly planned it mostly 16-mile days which are now too much for me even along the flat. About eight miles seems an ideal now and the twenty plus miles I was doing on the Pennine Way only four years ago seems a distant memory.

Gare du Nord on the way home

Old Hotel Ravel

Reception desk in Hotel Ravel

Citroën Traction Avant in Ceyrat

Summit Puy de Niermont (1620m)

Liqueur Artisanale Verveine

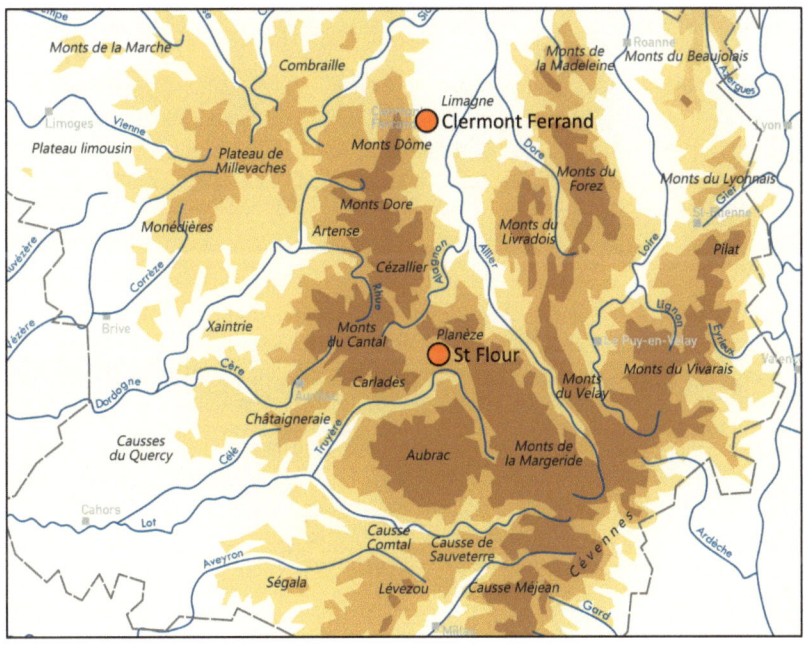

ITINERARY

1	Mon	29-Apr	Hathersage	London			Belgrove Hotel
2	Tue	30-Apr	London	St Flour			Grand Hotel L'Etape
3	Wed	01-May	St Flour	Prat de Bouc	28	17	Gîte Prat de Bouc
4	Thu	02-May	Prat de Bouc	Buron d'Eylac	18	11	Buron d'Eylac
5	Fri	03-May	Buron d'Eylac	Meynial Lugarde	24	15	Meynial Lugarde
6	Sat	04-May	Meynial Lugarde	Egliseneuve d'Entraigues	21	13	Auberge la Grange
7	Sun	05-May	Egliseneuve d'Entraigues	Mont Dore	26	16	Alti'Pic
8	Mon	06-May	Mont Dore	Lac de Cassiere	26	16	Entre Lacs y Volcan
9	Tue	07-May		Lac de Cassiere			Entre Lacs y Volcan
10	Wed	08-May		Clemont Ferrand			Old Hotel Ravel
11	Thu	09-May		Hathersage			
	Total				143	89	

KIT LIST

Item	Brand	Model/Detail	Notes	Qty	Value	Rating
Rucksack	Lightwave	Fastpac 30	Excellent, durable but very light. Could do with larger s	1	992	***
Rucksac cover	Lowe			1	63	**
First aid kit	Boots		Good, added compeed, second skin, arnica,	1	250	***
Note book	Moleskin		I always use these for my journals	1	111	***
Pens	Biro		Excellent	2	22	***
Phone	iPhone	12	Good battery life, excellent camera	1	75	***
Battery/cable	Anker	20000 mAh		1	322	**
Phone charger and adap	Apple			1	90	***
Head torch	Petzl	Light	and spare battery	1	36	***
Maps	Didier Richard	Corse du Nord	Excellent, very accurate, durable and easy to use	2	185	***
Compass	Silva	with whistle	Excellen, very practical, have always used Silva	1	42	***
Reading glasses				1	22	***
Pocket knife	Gerber	Paraframe		1	54	***
Debit card			Essential	1	1	
Dry bags	Sea to Summit	Assorted	Excellent, durable and completely waterproof	5	310	***
Walking poles	Black Diamond	Distance flz	Excellent, light and well balanced	2	384	***
Sandals	Crocs		Useful in camp for tired feet and for getting water fro	1	296	**
Water bottle	Platypus			1	71	**
Water bottle	Hydrapack			1	45	**
Pee bottle	Nalgene 1L			1	112	***
Lipsalve	Soltan	Factor 30		1	11	
Wash bag	CuraProX toothbrush			1	306	
Towels	Mountain Warehouse	Ex Large	Plus mini Go face towel	2	151	**
Lenses				1	122	
TOTAL KIT					4,073	
Boots	Sportiva		Wide fitting replacement boots bought in Corte	1	890	***
Gaiters	Sea to Summit		Good, light	1	110	**
Anorak	Arcteryx	Alpha SV	Orange	1	506	***
Fleece	Artilect		Windproof with hood	1	518	***
Cap	North Face			1	86	**
Gloves	Nike			1	61	**
Pants	Kühl		Excellent, fit well and good pockets	1	351	***
Pants	Royal Robbins			1	400	***
Shorts	Haglofs		Excellent, fit well and good pockets	1	299	***
T shirts	Adidas		Excellent, stayed looking smart	2	300	***
Leggings	Lowe		Gite wear	1	20	***
Gilet	Mammut		Emergency wear and used at A Sega Gite	1	415	
Socks	Bridgedale		Excellent, very comfortable	2	0	
Underpants	M&S			2	46	
Swimming trunks	Speedo				90	***
Belt	Jukmo	Ratchet belt	Essential, because you loose weight (6-7 kilos)	1	25	***
TOTAL CLOTHES					4,117	
TOTAL					8,190	

TRAINING WALKS

Date	Title	Area	Miles	Km	Ascent
09/07/2022	Stanton Moor	Peak	2	3	100
07/07/2023	Dovestones	Holmfirth	6	10	1,573
29/07/2023	Millpond	Stanage	4	6	650
16/08/2023	Witherslack	Lakes	6.4	10	780
15/09/2023	Hull	Saltholme RSPB	3	5	20
22/09/2023	Melmerby Fell	Teesdale	9.7	16	1,919
23/09/2023	Crossfell	Kirkland	9	14	2,440
24/09/2023	Hadrian's Wall	Once Brewed-	4.6	7	600
11/11/2023	Blackden Clough	Kinder	6	10	1,900
26/12/2023	Camp Hill	Peak	6	10	1,600
01/01/2024	Eyam Moor	Peak	4	6	987
04/01/2024	Cheviot	Rothbury	6.3	10	2,067
05/01/2024	Lamb Hill	Blindburn	7.2	12	1,355
06/01/2024	Holy Island	Lindisfarne	5	8	10
09/02/2024	Formby	Ainsdale	5	8	215
14/02/2024	Burbage	Peak	4.0	6.4	532
18/03/2024	Stanage Callow	Peak	2.0	3.2	200
14/04/2024	Rushup Edge	Peak	4.0	6.4	753
Total			94	152	17,701

www.ingramcontent.com/pod-product-compliance
Lightning Source LLC
Chambersburg PA
CBHW042306150426
43197CB00001B/28